BIRDS

A PICTURE SOURCEBOOK

EDITED AND ARRANGED BY DON RICE

Over 600 copyright-free illustrations
for direct copying and reference

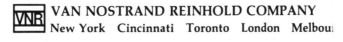

VAN NOSTRAND REINHOLD COMPANY
New York Cincinnati Toronto London Melbou

Published in 1980 by Van Nostrand Reinhold Company
A division of Litton Educational Publishing, Inc.
135 West 50th Street, New York, NY 10020, U.S.A.

Van Nostrand Reinhold Limited
1410 Birchmount Road
Scarborough, Ontario M1P 2E7, Canada

Van Nostrand Reinhold Australia Pty. Ltd.
17 Queen Street
Mitcham, Victoria 3132, Australia

Van Nostrand Reinhold Company Limited
Molly Millars Lane
Wokingham, Berkshire, England

16 15 14 13 12 11 10 9 8 7 6 5 4 3 2 1

Library of Congress Cataloging in Publication Data

Main entry under title:

Birds, a picture sourcebook

Includes index.
1. Birds in art.   2 Birds — Pictorial works.
I. Rice, Donald L.
N7665-B48

I. Rice, Donald L.
N7665-B48   760   04432   80-14849
ISBN 0-442-20395-0 (pbk.)

Introduction

The illustrations in this collection were drawn or engraved over a period of 100 years, from the early 1800s to the early 1900s, by innumerable artists demonstrating a wide variety of skills, styles, and knowledge about their subjects. Many are beautifully executed and very accurate. Some, such as the eagle flying off with the young girl, are quite fanciful. All have useful applications for artists, students, and researchers. The collection is intended to serve as three books in one:

Clip Book

Up to 10 illustrations may be copied directly for each graphic arts project without obtaining further permission from the publisher. A credit line, though not necessary, would be appreciated.

Source Book

As a portable artist's "swipe file" it will provide a handy guide in the creation of original drawings and paintings of birds.

Reference Book

The birds pictured are alphabetically categorized first by order (indicated by a solid black line), then by family (broken line), and then by species (with occasional lapses in alphabetizing to accommodate page layouts). It seemed unnecessary for the purposes of this book to divide the families into subfamilies and genera.

Birds were not systematically classified to any reasonable degree until Linnaeus published the 10th edition of his *Systema Naturae* in 1785. Since that time there have been radical changes in the approaches to scientific classification. One might suppose that by now the science of systematics would be an exhausted field, and that the classifications would be chiseled in stone. But this is far from being true. The approach to classification has broadened greatly in recent years, and revisions are constantly being made.

For example, if one were to look up the avocet in reference book A, one would find it listed as a member of the family *Recurvirostridae*. In reference book B, however, one would discover that this family had been reduced to a subfamily *(Recurvirostrinae)* within the family *Charadriidae*. The latter is the more recent, and that is the classification that has been used for this book. It is highly possible that some readers will disagree with some of the choices that have been made in this regard. Readers may also find what they consider to be some out-and-out mistakes. They are encouraged to bring these to my attention by writing to the publisher.

Don Rice

Contents

Nest Building

Expectation

Feeding the Young

A Snug Retreat

Brant

Canada Goose

Bufflehead Duck

Canvas-back

Canada Goose

Cape Barren Goose

Eider Duck

Emperor Goose

Eider Duck

Eider Duck

Graylag Goose

Goldeneye

Gadwall

Labrador Duck

Mallard

Mallard

Mallard

Merganser

Mallard

Red-breasted Merganser

Old Squaw

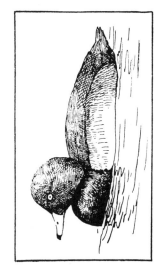

Redhead

American Scaup

Greater Scaup

Surf Scoter

Black Scoter

Shoveller-duck

Black-necked Swan

Black Swan

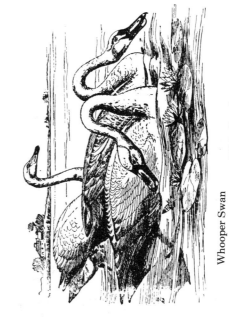

Whooper Swan

Whistling Swan

Trumpeter Swan

Whooper Swan

Swan

Whooper Swan

Shoveller-duck

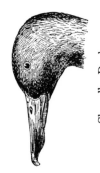

Shoveller-Duck

Blue-winged Teal

Blue-winged Teal

Green-winged Teal

Green-winged Teal

Widgeon

Teal

Widgeon

Widgeon

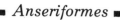

Anatidae

Wood Duck

Wood Duck

Wood Duck

Anhimidae

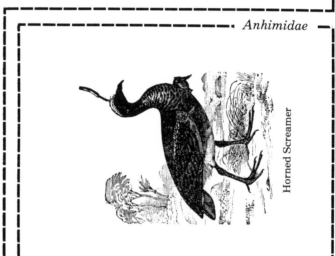

Horned Screamer

Apodiformes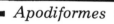

Apodidae

Chimney Swift

Swift

9

Apodidae

Trochilidae

Salangane

Coquette Hummingbird

Ruby-throat Hummingbird

Sicklebill Hummingbird

Ruby-throat Hummingbird

Ruby-throat Hummingbird

Hummingbirds

Hummingbirds

Apterygiformes

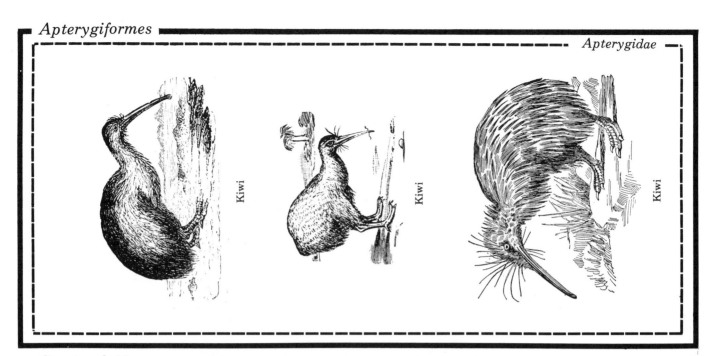

Kiwi

Kiwi

Kiwi

Caprimulgiformes

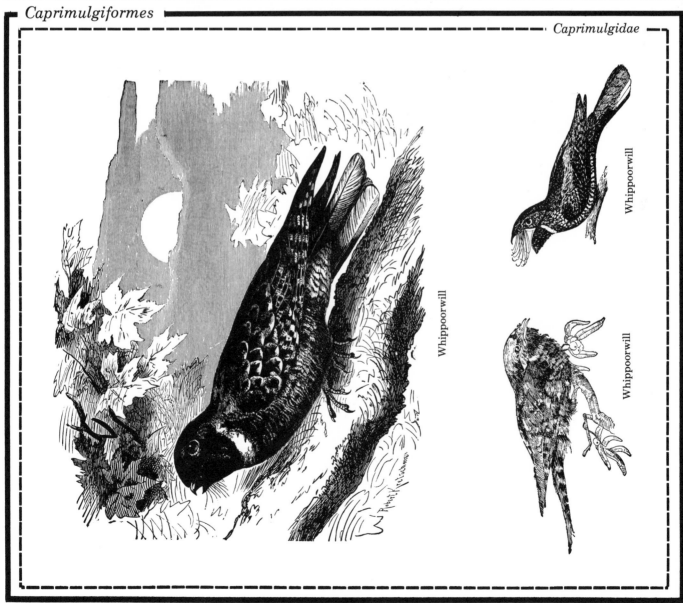

Whippoorwill

Whippoorwill

Whippoorwill

Nightjar

Caprimulgidae

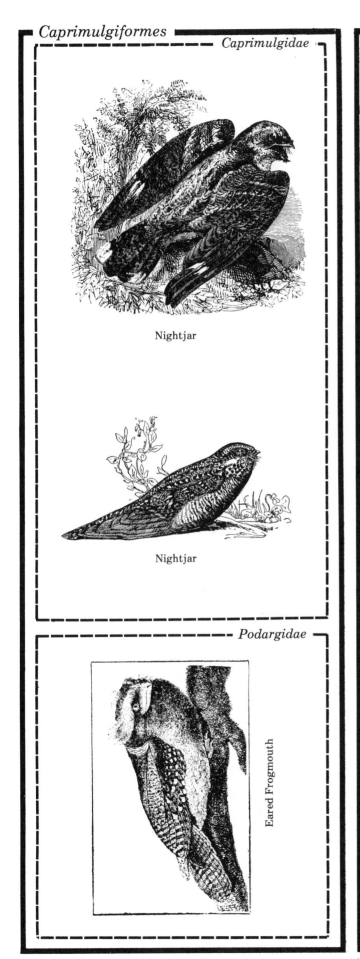

Nightjar

Nightjar

Podargidae

Eared Frogmouth

Casuariidae

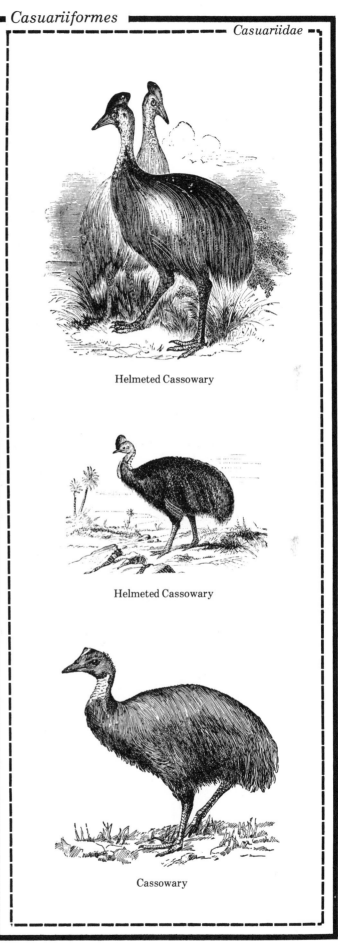

Helmeted Cassowary

Helmeted Cassowary

Cassowary

Cassowary

Dromiceiidae

Alcidae

Emu

Emu

Emu

Dovekie

Puffin

Puffin

Tufted Puffin

Horned Puffin

Alcidae

Great Auk

Great Auk

Great Auk

Crested Auk

Burhinidae

Thickknee

Charadriidae

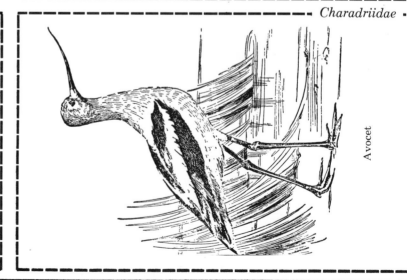

Avocet

Curlew

European Avocet

Old World Curlew

Curlew

Dotterel

Dotterel

Godwit

Killdeer

Hudsonian Godwit

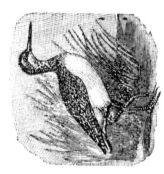

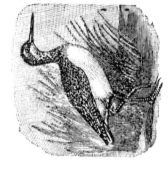

Greenshank

Knot

Lapwing

Lapwing

Lapwing

Crookbill Plover

Grey Plover

Ring Plover

Golden Plover

Semipalmated Plover

Spur-winged Plover

Redshank

Reeve

Ruff

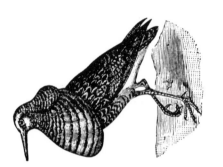

Ruff

Ruff

Snipe

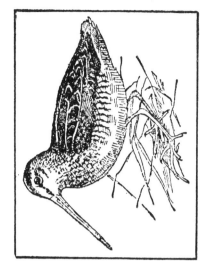

Wilson's Snipe

Turnstone

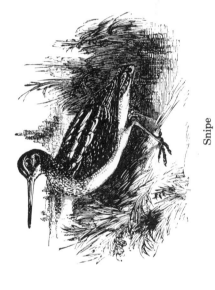

Snipe

Turnstone

Charadriiformes

Chionididae

Small Sheathbill

Larger Sheathbill

Glareolidae

Sicsac

Haematopodidae

American Oyster-catcher

Laridae

Kittiwake

Jacanidae

Jacana

Mexican Jacana

Asiatic Jacana

Great Black-backed Gull

Ross's Gull

Great Black-backed Gull

Gull

Great Black-headed Gull

Tern

Black Tern

Charadriiformes

Laridae

Tern

Caspian Tern

Tern

Rynchopidae

Black Skimmer

Black Skimmer

Scolopacidae

Dunlin

Pectoral Sandpiper

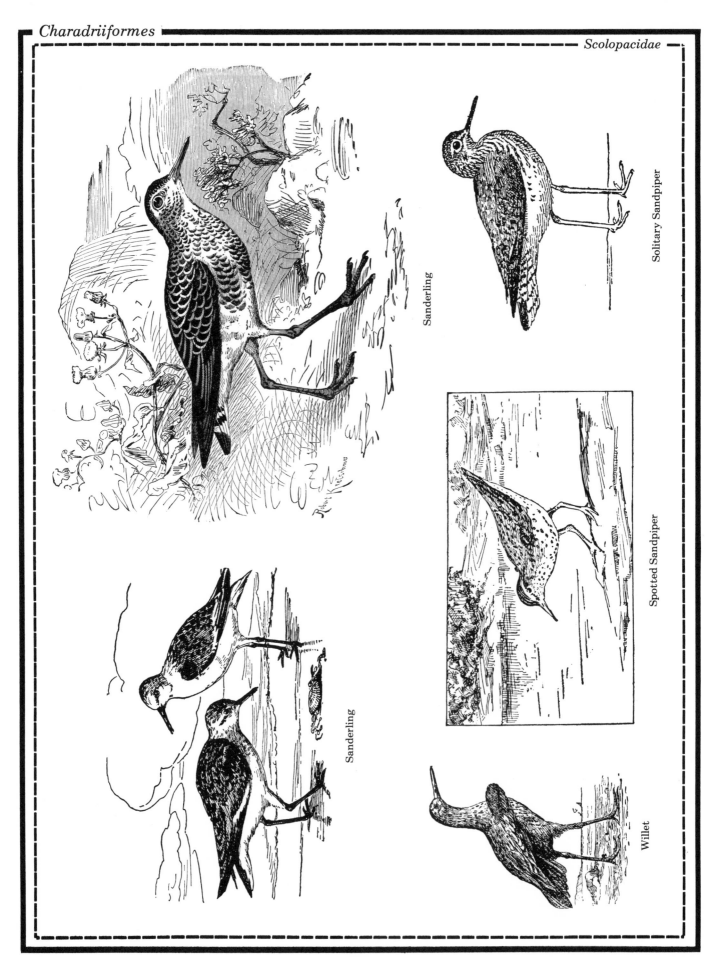

Sanderling

Solitary Sandpiper

Sanderling

Spotted Sandpiper

Willet

Woodcock

Woodcock

Woodcock

Yellowlegs

Lesser Yellowlegs

Greater Yellowlegs

Skua

Bittern

Bittern

Bittern

American Bittern

Brazilian Sun Bittern

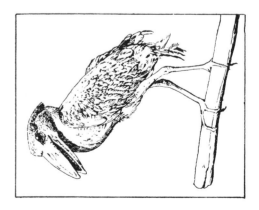

Boatbill

Little White Egret

Great Blue Heron

Snowy Heron

Heron

Herons

Great Blue Heron

Yellow-crowned Night-heron

Balaenicipitidae

Shoebill

Great White Egret

33

Shoebill

Adjutant

Adjutant

Adjutant

Jabiru

White Stork

Stork

Openbill

Simbil

Wood-ibis

Glossy Ibis　　　Sacred Ibis

Ibis

European Spoonbill

Ciconiiformes

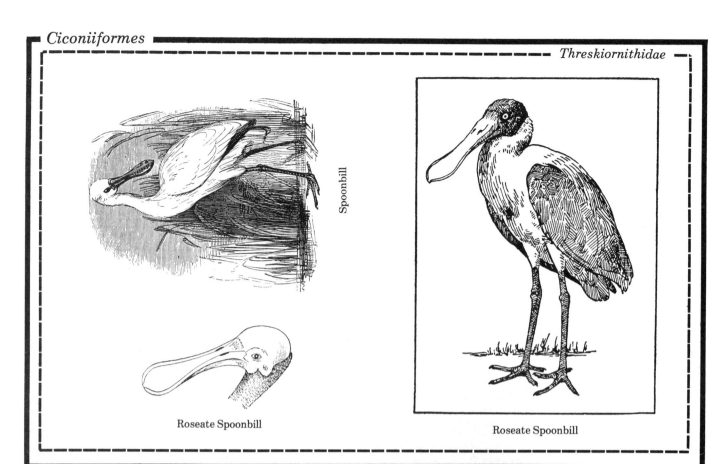

Spoonbill

Roseate Spoonbill

Roseate Spoonbill

Coliiformes

Coliidae

Mousebird

Columbiformes

Columbidae

Blue-headed Pigeon

Crowned Pigeon

Bronze-wing Pigeon

Carrier Pigeon

Ground Dove

Mourning Dove

Passenger Pigeon

Pouter Pigeon

Rock Pigeon

Turtledoves

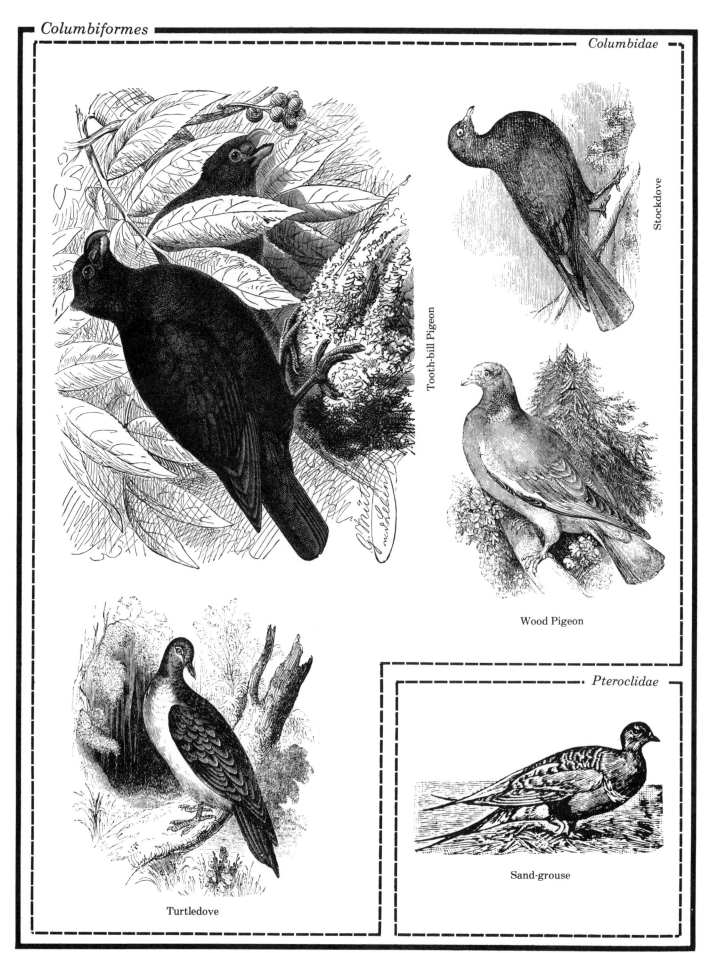

Stockdove

Tooth-bill Pigeon

Wood Pigeon

Pteroclidae

Turtledove

Sand-grouse

Belted Kingfisher

Kingfisher

Belted Kingfisher

Kingfisher

Kookaburra Kingfisher

Papuan Hornbill

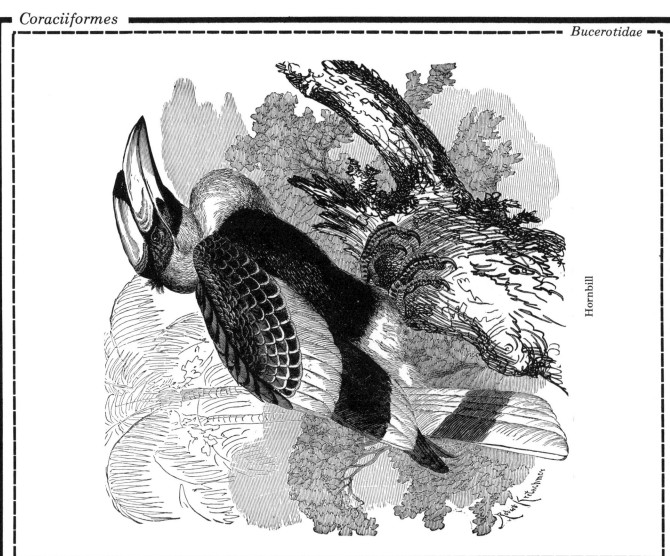

Hornbill

Coraciidae

Momotidae

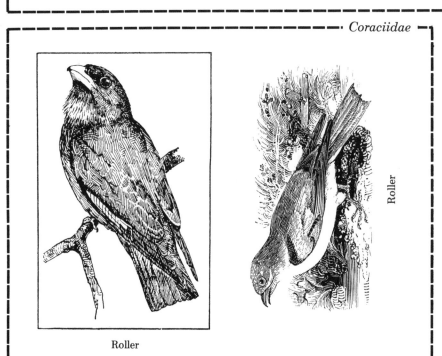

Roller

Roller

Motmot

Coraciiformes

Todidae

Cuban Tody

Upupidae

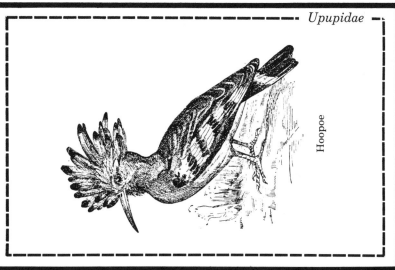

Hoopoe

Cuculiformes

Cuculidae

Smooth-billed Ani

Cuckoo

Cuckoo

Cuckoo

Roadrunner

Musophagidae

Roadrunner

Plaintain Eater

European Buzzard

Rough-legged Hawk

Honey Buzzard

Bald Eagle

Bald Eagle

Bald Eagle

Bald Eagle

Eagle

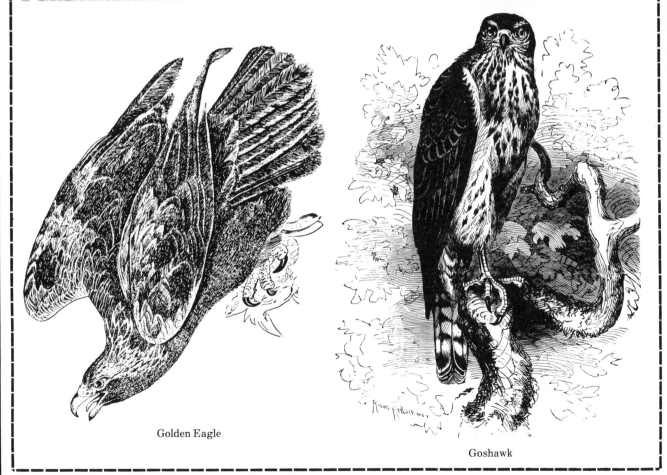

Golden Eagle

Goshawk

Steller's Sea-Eagle

Hen Harrier

Eastern Red-tailed Hawk

Goshawk

Red-shouldered Hawk

Marsh Hawk

Sharp-shinned Hawk

Mississippi Kite   Swallow-tailed Kite

Mississippi Kite

Lammergeier

Red Kite

Egyptian Vulture

Common Kite

Turkey Vulture

Turkey Vulture

Turkey Vulture

Andean Condor

California Condor

Condor

Cathartidae

Black Vulture

Condor

Falconidae

Urubu

Audubon Caracara

Vulture

Peregrine Falcon

Peregrine Falcon

American Sparrow Hawk

Peregrine Falcon

Gyrfalcon

Falcons

Osprey

Osprey

Osprey

Osprey

Secretary Bird

Secretary Bird

Guan

Galeated Curassow

Chacalaca

Rooster

Hen and Chicks

Silver-spangled Hamburgs

Rooster

Silver Sebright Bantams

Black-breasted Red Games

Japanese Bantams

Pit games

Indian Games

La Fleche

White Leghorns

Black Langshans

Buff Cochins

Partridge Cochins

Light Brahmas

Mottled Javas

Barred Plymouth Rocks

Silver-laced Wyandottes

Silver-gray Dorkings

White-faced Black Spanish

Houdans

Black Minorcas

White-crested Black Polish

Megapodiidae

Mound-bird

Meleagrididae

Turkey

Turkey

Ocellated Turkey

Turkey

Galliformes

Numididae

Guinea Fowl

Opisthocomidae

Hoazin

Phasianidae

Chukar

Francolin

Gambel's Partridge

Red-legged Partridge

Peacock

Peacock

Reeve's Pheasant

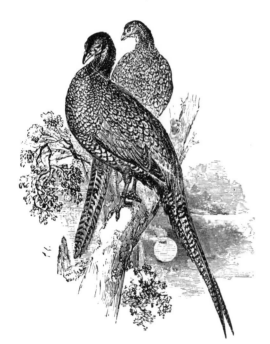

Pheasant

Golden Pheasant

English Ring-neck Pheasant

Impeyan Pheasant

Many-colored Golden Pheasant

Argus Pheasant

Lady Amherst Pheasant

European Quail

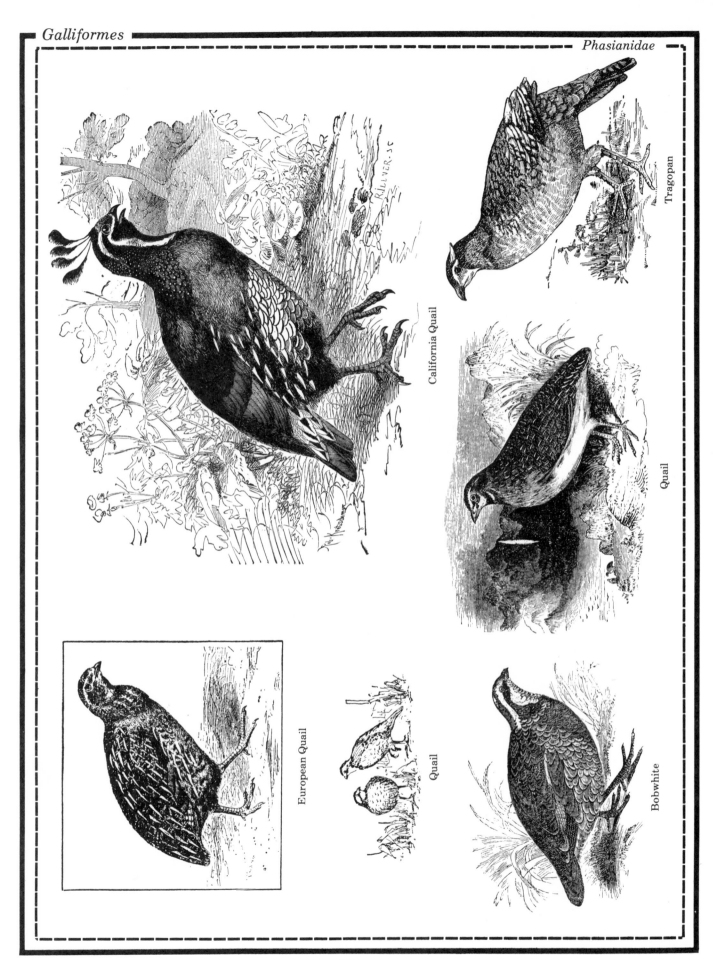

Tragopan

California Quail

Quail

European Quail

Quail

Bobwhite

Capercaillie

Capercaillie

Ruffed Grouse

Black Cock

Red Grouse

Ruffed Grouse

Sage Grouse

Siberian Wood Grouse

Willow Ptarmigan

Ptarmigan

Ptarmigan

Prairie Chicken

Prairie Chicken

Ptarmigan

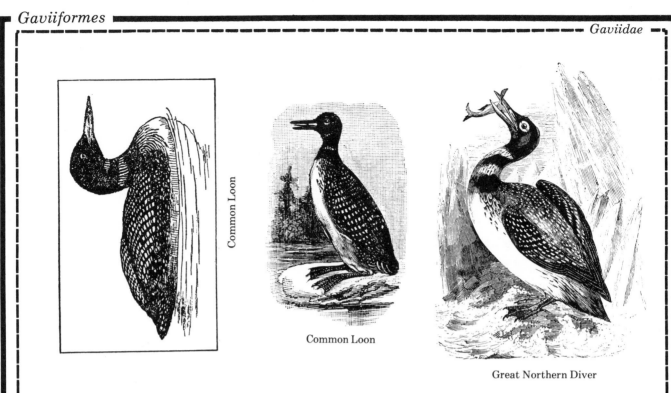

Common Loon

Common Loon

Great Northern Diver

Gruiformes

Aramidae

Gruidae

Limpkin

Cariamidae

Seriema

Crane

Gruidae

Crane

Demoiselle Crane

Heliornithidae

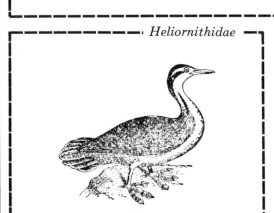

Sun-grebe

Otididae

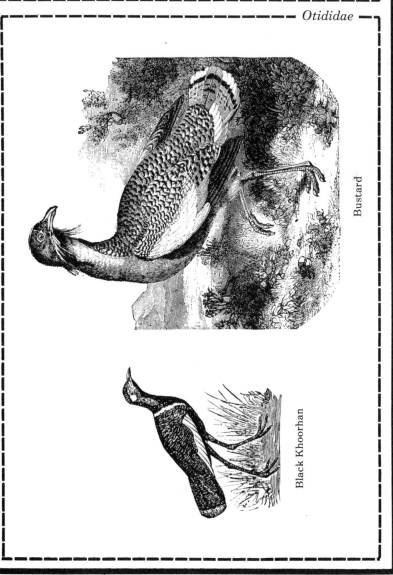

Bustard

Black Khoorhan

Psophiidae

Trumpeter

Moorcock

Coot

American Coot

American Coot

Corncrake

Sora

Water-hen

Prairie Horned Lark

Skylark

Northern Horned Lark

Woodlark

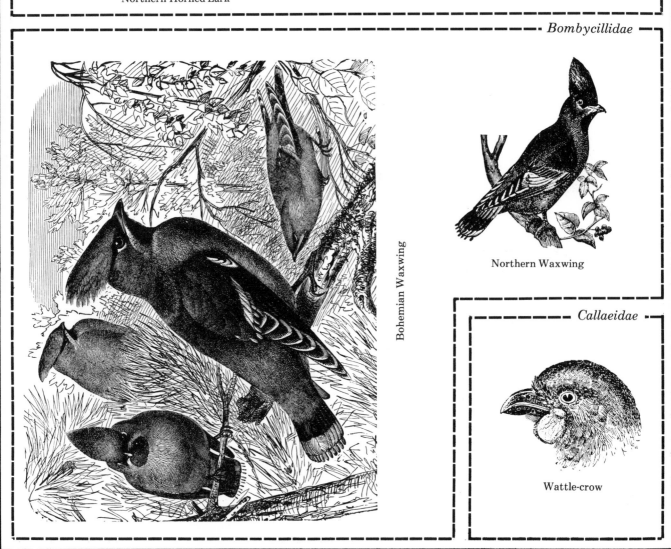

Bohemian Waxwing

Northern Waxwing

Wattle-crow

Huia-bird

Certhiidae

Brown Creeper

Cinclidae

North American Dipper

Cinclidae

Compsothlypidae

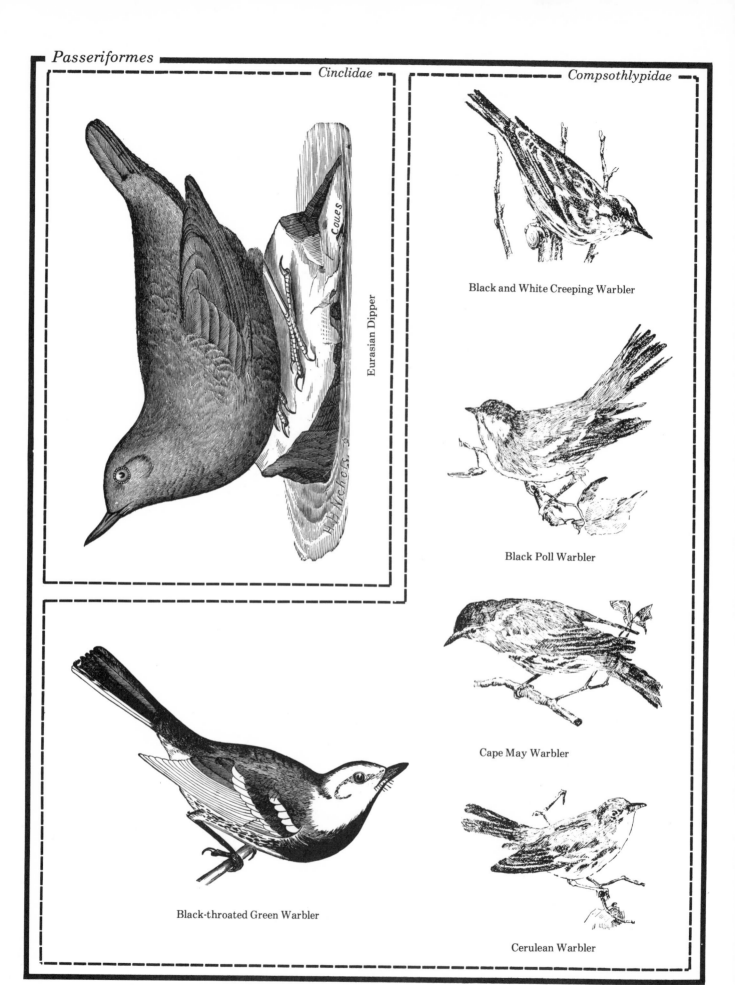

Eurasian Dipper

Black and White Creeping Warbler

Black Poll Warbler

Cape May Warbler

Black-throated Green Warbler

Cerulean Warbler

Warblers

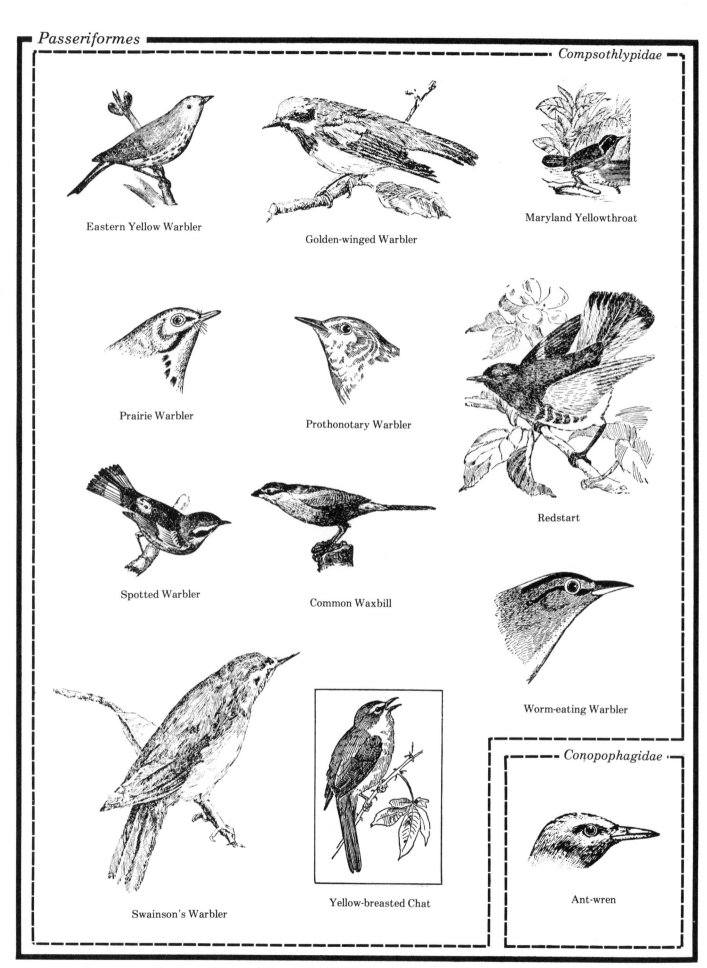

Eastern Yellow Warbler

Golden-winged Warbler

Maryland Yellowthroat

Prairie Warbler

Prothonotary Warbler

Redstart

Spotted Warbler

Common Waxbill

Worm-eating Warbler

Conopophagidae

Swainson's Warbler

Yellow-breasted Chat

Ant-wren

Carrion Crow

American Blue Jay

Blue Jay

Crow

Cornish Chough

Chough

Crows

Carrion Crow

Jackdaw

Jackdaw

Jay

Magpie

Canada Jay

Pinon Jay

Green Magpie

Raven

Raven

Ravens

Corvidae

Rook

Temia

Cotingidae

Amazon Bellbird

Cotinga

Cock of the Rock

Naked-throated Bellbird

Dicruridae

Drongo

Black-headed Bunting

Yellowhammer

Passeriformes

Emberizidae

Buntings

Ortolan Bunting

Estrildidae

Senegal

Eurylamidae

Broadbill

Fringillidae

Bullfinch

Brambling

Canary-bird

Chaffinch

Cardinal

Crossbill

Crossbill

Goldfinch

American Goldfinch

Rose-breasted Grosbeak

Slate-colored Junco

Cardinal

Rose-breasted Grosbeak

Linnet

Indigo Bunting

Linnet

European Siskin

Little Seed-eater

American Tree-sparrow

Savanna Sparrow

Swamp Sparrow

Vesper Sparrow

White-throated Sparrow

Song Sparrow

Towhee

Yellow Warbler

Spanish Sparrow

White-throated Sparrow

Sparrows

Ovenbird

Swallow

Swallow

House Martin

Bank Swallow

Fairy Martin

Barn Swallow

Northern Oriole

Bobolink

Northern Oriole

Northern Oriole Nest

Great Crested Cacique

Bobolink

Bobolink

Cowbird

Meadowlark

Meadowlark

Purple Grackle

Red-winged Blackbird

Yellowhead Blackbird

Savanna Blackbird

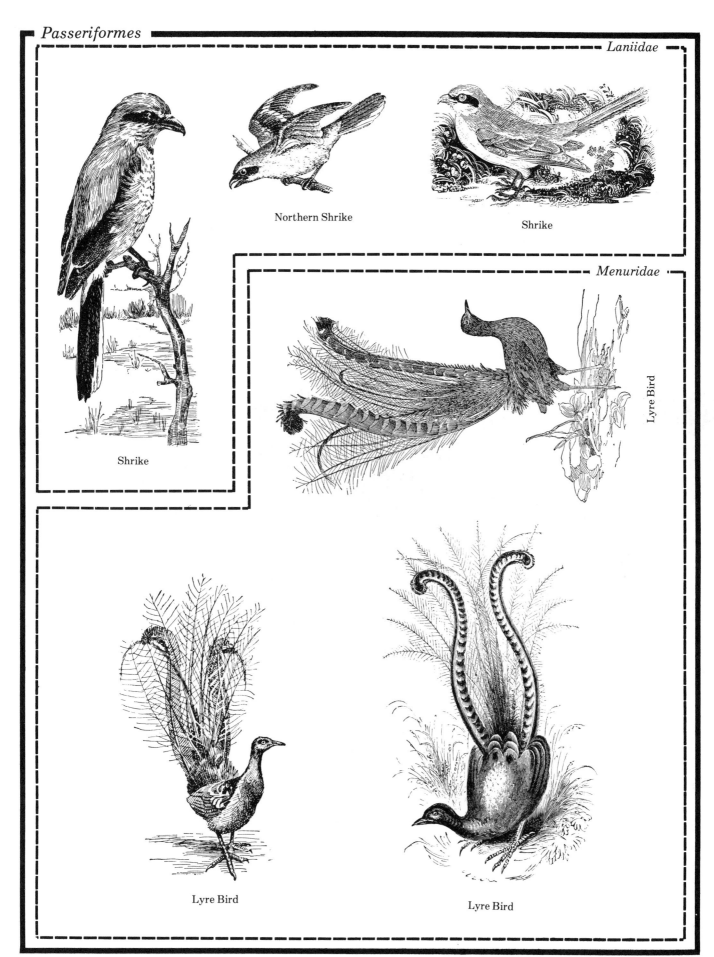

Northern Shrike

Shrike

Menuridae

Lyre Bird

Shrike

Lyre Bird

Lyre Bird

Lyre Bird

Mocking Bird

Brown Thrasher

Catbird

Mocking Bird

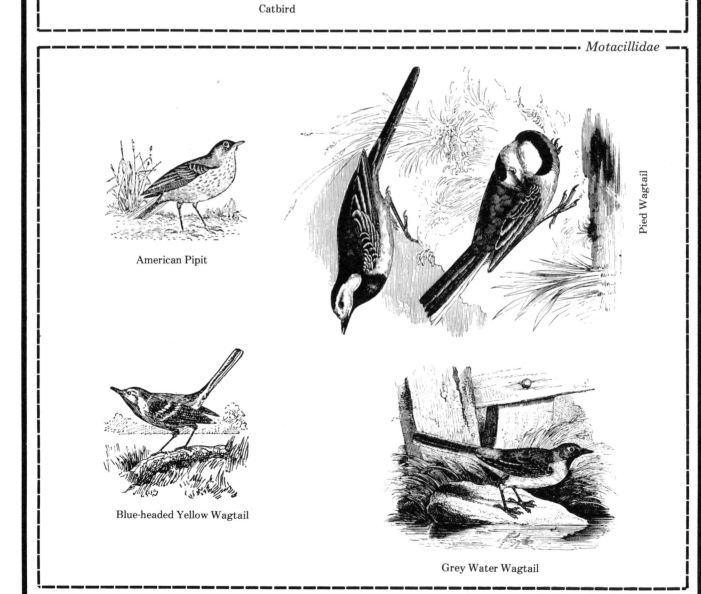

American Pipit

Pied Wagtail

Blue-headed Yellow Wagtail

Grey Water Wagtail

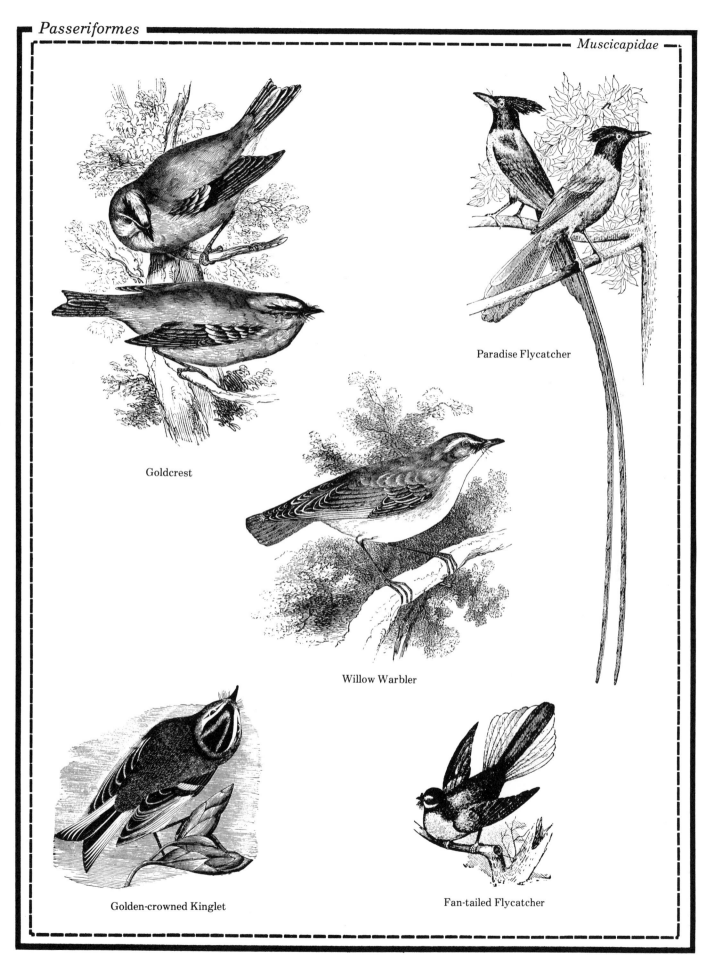

Goldcrest

Paradise Flycatcher

Willow Warbler

Golden-crowned Kinglet

Fan-tailed Flycatcher

Sunbird

Great Bird of Paradise

Six-shafted Bird of Paradise

Great Bird of Paradise

Wilson's Bird of Paradise

King Bird of Paradise

King of Saxony Bird of Paradise

Titmouse

Long-tailed Tit

Blue Tit

Black-capped Chickadee

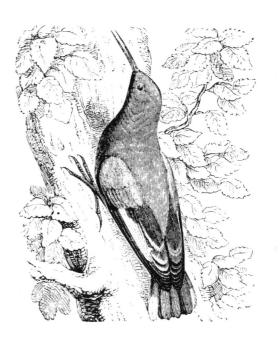

Wall Creeper

Bush Tit

Verdin

Phytotomidae

Chilean Plant-cutter

Pittidae

Pitta

Ploceidae

Social Weaver

Weaver Bird Nests

Red-billed Quella

English Sparrows

Paradise Whydah

English Sparrow

Dunnock

Satin Bower Bird

Regent Bower Bird

White-breasted Nuthatch

Satin Bower Bird

Red-breasted Nuthatch

White-breasted Nuthatch

Magpie *(Corvidae* family)

Starlings

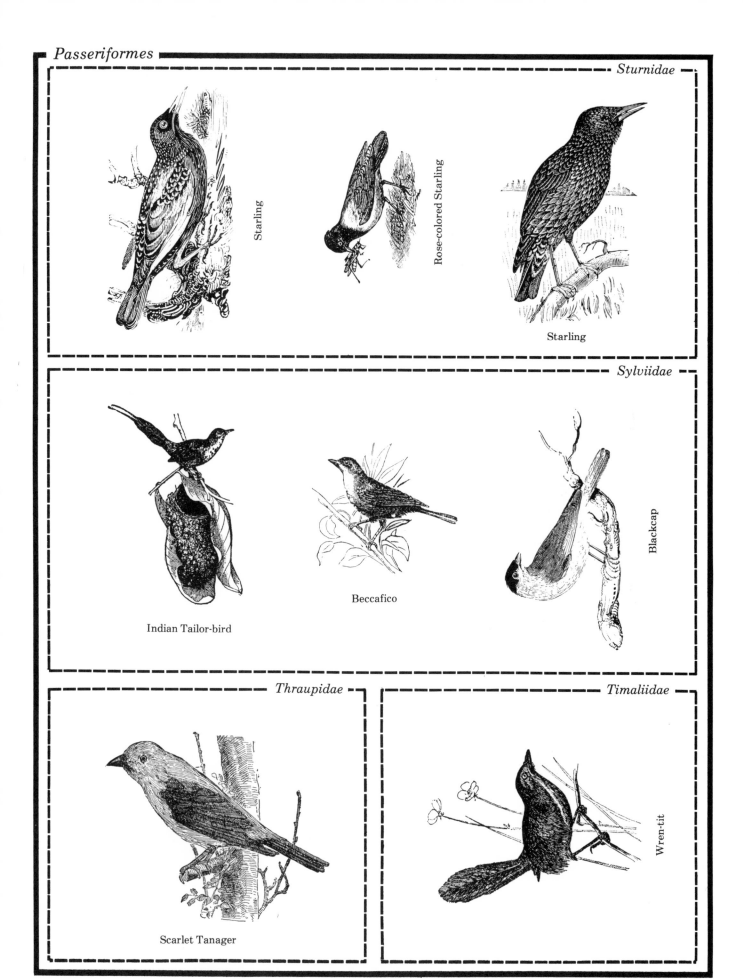

Passeriformes

Sturnidae

Starling

Rose-colored Starling

Starling

Sylviidae

Indian Tailor-bird

Beccafico

Blackcap

Thraupidae

Scarlet Tanager

Timaliidae

Wren-tit

Troglodytidae

Turdidae

House Wren

Short-billed Marsh Wren

Long-billed Marsh Wren

1. Cactus Wren

2. Canon Wren

Wren

Blackbird

Bluebird

Fieldfare

Nightingale

Nightingale

Redwing

Ring Ouzel

American Robin

American Robin

Northern Varied Thrush

American Robin

Stonechat

Missel Thrush

Wood Thrush

Passeriformes

Turdidae

Tyrannidae

Wheatear
Whinchat

Veery

Fire-crowned Tyrant

Eastern Kingbird

Phoebe

Scissortail Flycatcher

Eastern Kingbird

Wood Pewee

Spotted Flycatcher

Passeriformes

Vangidae

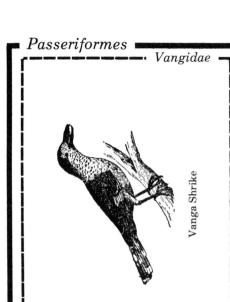

Vanga Shrike

Vireonidae

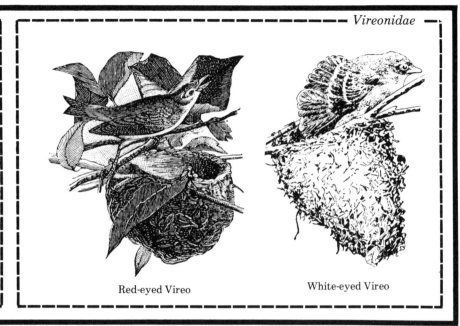

Red-eyed Vireo

White-eyed Vireo

Pelecaniformes

Anhingidae

Indian Darter

Indian Darter

Fregatidae

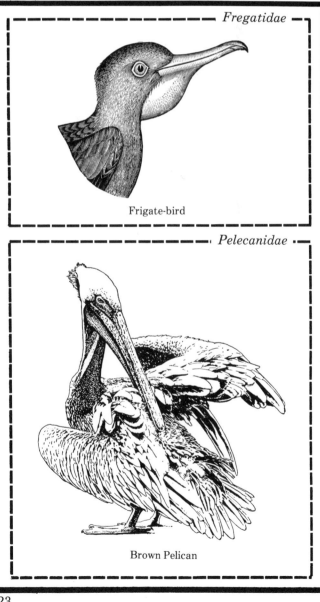

Frigate-bird

Pelecanidae

Brown Pelican

White Pelican

Phaethontidae

Red-billed Tropic-bird

White Pelican

Red-billed Tropic-bird

Shag

Common Cormorant

Gannet

Gannet

Flamingo

Flamingo

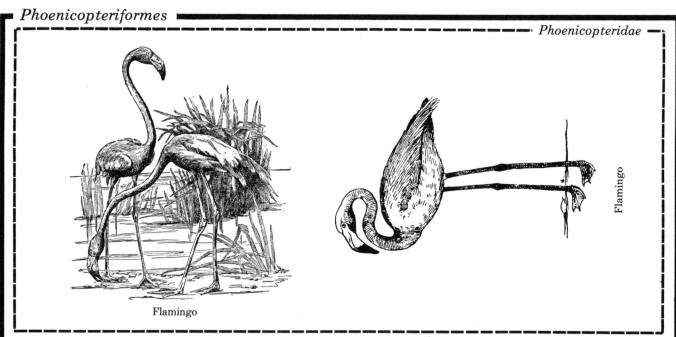

Phoenicopteridae

Flamingo

Flamingo

Flamingo

Piciformes

Picidae

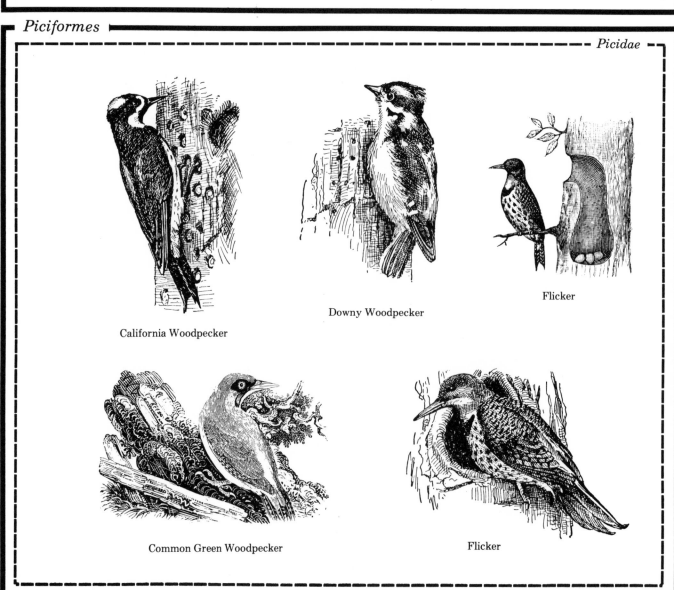

California Woodpecker

Downy Woodpecker

Flicker

Common Green Woodpecker

Flicker

Downy Woodpecker

Ivory-billed Woodpecker

Pileated Woodpecker

Red-bellied Woodpecker

Red-headed Woodpecker

Wryneck

Yellow-bellied Sapsucker

Wryneck

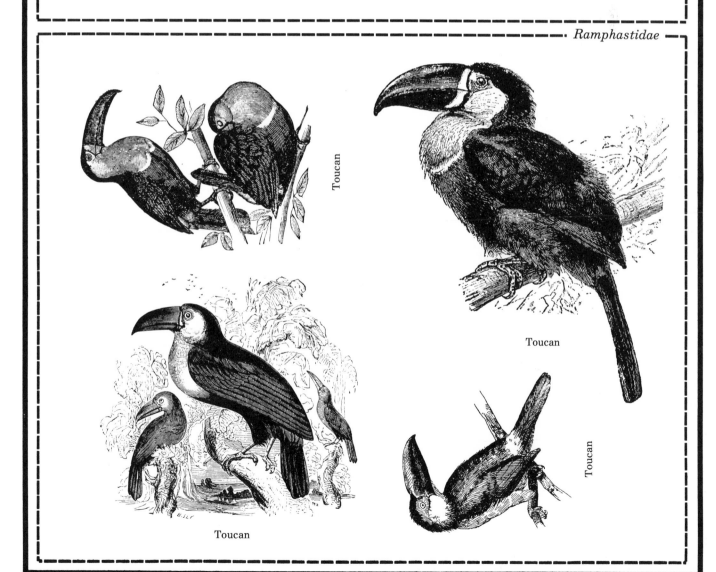

Toucan

Toucan

Toucan

Toucan

Least Grebe

Podicepediformes

Crested Grebe

Grebe

Procellariiformes

Sooty Albatross

Wandering Albatross

Hydrobatidae

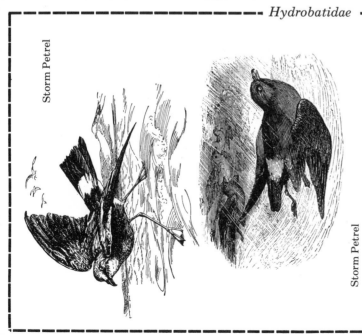

Storm Petrel

Storm Petrel

Procellariidae

Fulmar

Rose-crested Cockatoo

Sulpher-crested Cockatoo

Lovebird

Kaka

Lory

Pink Cockatoo

Kea

Blue and Yellow Macaw

Macaw

Grass Parakeet

Carolina Parakeet

Parakeet

Parrot

Pigmy Parrot

Gray Parrot

Ring Parrot

137

Macaw

Rhea

Rhea

Rhea

Emperor Penguin

Galapagos Penguin

Jackass Penguin

King Penguin

Burrowing Owl

Tawny Owl

Eagle Owl

Snowy Owl

Great Horned Owl

Gnome Owl

Horned Owl

Screech Owl

Tytonidae

Snowy Owl

Barn Owl

Ostrich

Ostrich

Ostrich

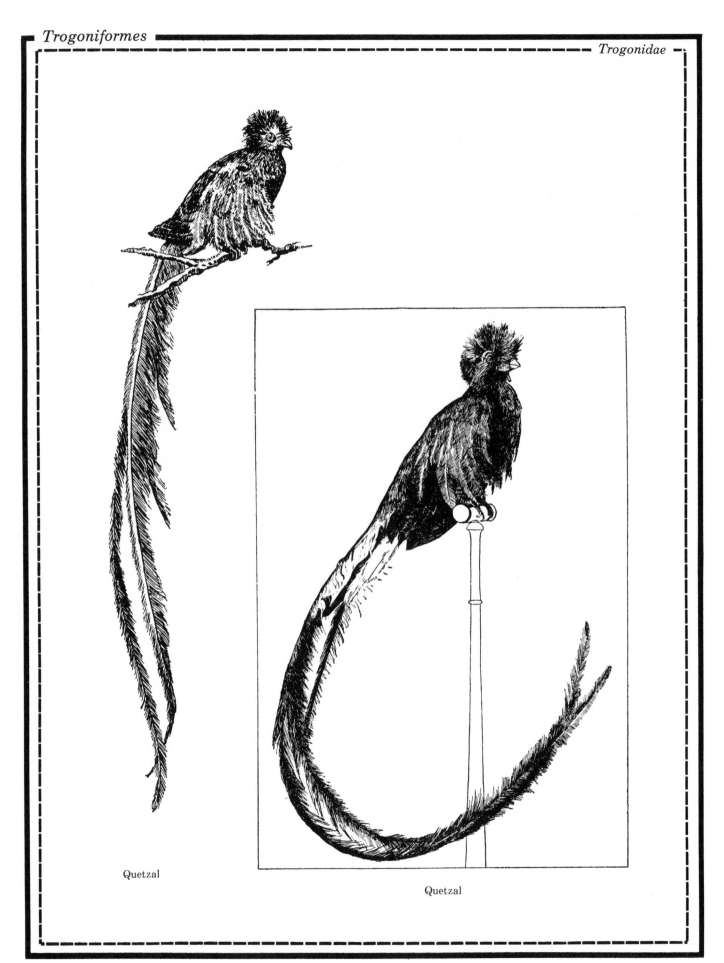

Quetzal

Quetzal

Index

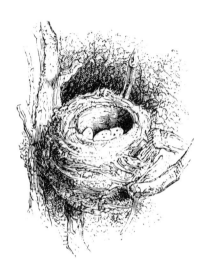

At different times and in different places an individual species of bird may often be known by various names. Some birds seem especially to stimulate the imagination of folk-taxonomists. The Old Squaw, a member of the duck family *(Anatidae)*, has been known as Calloo, Cockawee, John Connolly, Coween, Long-tail Duck, Swallow-tailed Duck, Hound, Old Billy, Old Granny, Old Injun, Old Molly, Old Wife, Quanty, Scoldenore, Scolder, South-southerly, and Uncle Huldy. Other species have had — and continue to have — even a greater number of different names. As an aid to the reader, nearly 500 such names have been cross-indexed here.

149